AN A-MAZE-ING SCHOOL ADVENTURE

BY JILL KALZ   ILLUSTRATED BY MATTIA CERATO

PICTURE WINDOW BOOKS
a capstone imprint

Designer: Lori Bye
Art Director: Nathan Gassman
Production Specialist: Jane Klenk
The illustrations in this book were created digitally.

Picture Window Books
151 Good Counsel Drive
P.O. Box 669
Mankato, MN 56002-0669
877-845-8392
www.capstonepub.com

All books published by Picture Window Books
are manufactured with paper containing at least
10 percent post-consumer waste.

Library of Congress Cataloging-in-Publication Data

Kalz, Jill.
  An a-maze-ing school adventure / by Jill Kalz ; illustrated
by Mattia Cerato.
       p. cm. — (A-maze-ing adventures)
  Includes index.
  ISBN 978-1-4048-6039-1 (library binding)
  1. Schools—Juvenile literature. 2. Maze puzzles—Juvenile
literature. 3. Map reading—Juvenile literature. I. Cerato, Mattia,
ill. II. Title.
  LB1513.K367 2011
  371—dc22
                              2010018122

Printed in the United States of America in North Mankato, Minnesota.
012011   006057R

WELCOME TO THE
A-MAZE-ING SCHOOL

Here's what you do: Use your finger to make your way through each maze from start to finish. If a person, chair, or other object blocks your way, choose a different path. It's **OK** to use the stairs and ladders. The star in the lower left corner of each maze shows direction. It's called a compass rose. The boxes with tiny pictures are called keys or legends. They'll help you find art supplies, books, field day events, and more.

What's that frisky guinea pig up to? See if you can spot him sneaking through each maze.

Answers start on page 26.

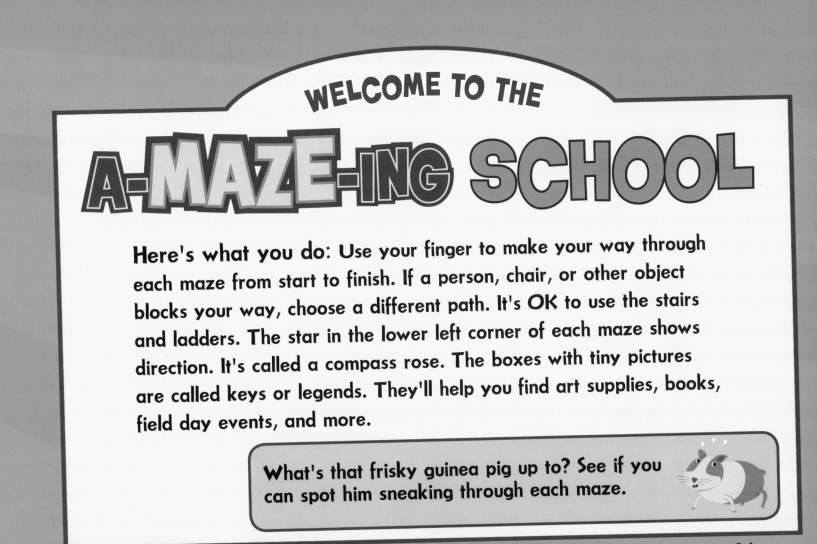

Hooray for Homeroom!

Can you find your way through this mess of desks? Which direction is the Start door from the Finish door? Is the globe north or south of the pink backpack? Can you spot the other six backpacks?

START

4

FINISH

5

START

HOT!

6

Lost in the Lab

Ready to do some experiments? Step one: Use the key to find your gear. Step two: Find your chemicals and tools. Step three: Strap on your goggles, and measure and mix up some science fun!

FINISH

KEY

- Gear
- Tools
- Chemicals
- HOT! Oven

HOT!

Read All about It

Discover magic in the media center—but quietly, please! Use the key to find the fiction, nonfiction, and reference book sections. Are the audio/visual cases north or south of the storyteller? West or east of the games?

START

8

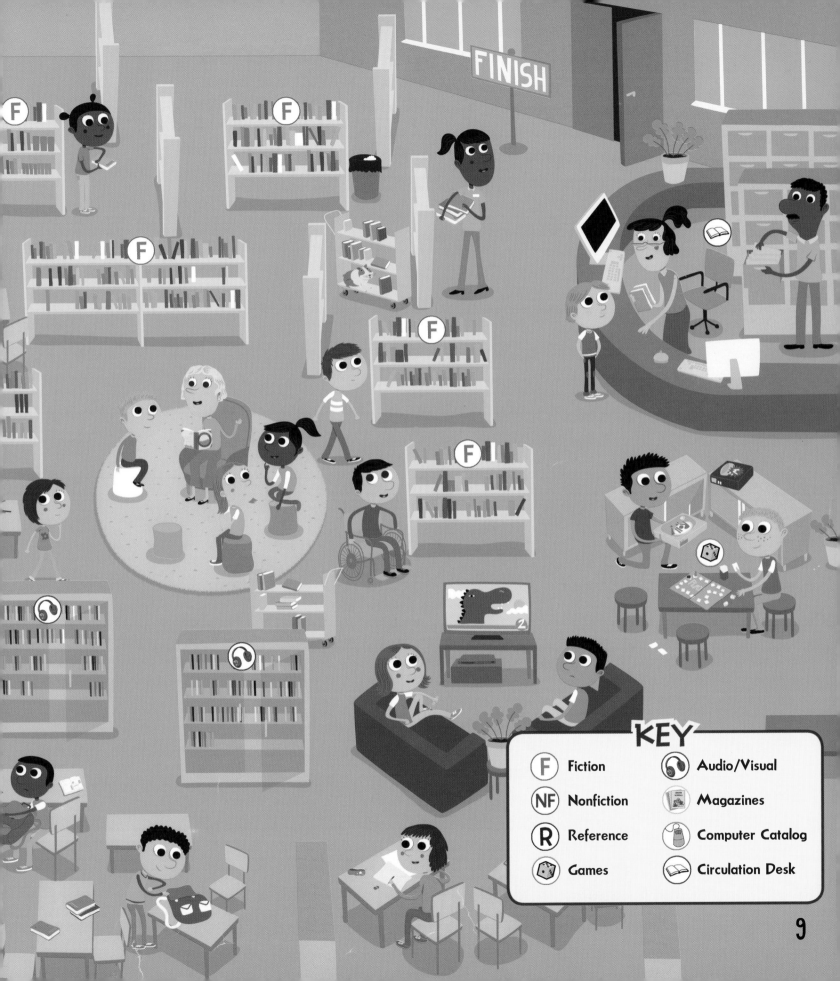

FINISH

KEY

F Fiction

NF Nonfiction

R Reference

Games

Audio/Visual

Magazines

Computer Catalog

Circulation Desk

9

Balls, Walls, Nets, and Beams

Time to tumble and twist. Catch and climb. Bounce, balance, and bump. If you're standing at the volleyball net, which direction should you go to get to the climbing wall? To the yellow beams? Can you find all 21 balls? (And don't worry; you *can* cross the white lines on the floor to get to the Finish!)

START

FINISH

Take Your Seat

Lots of empty seats in the auditorium, but only one is yours. Once you get to the Finish, see if you can spot the two students taking a nap.

START

12

Who's Hungry?

Is that your stomach growling? Let's eat! Is the lunch counter west or east of the recycling bins? Which direction are the trash bins from the boy with the football? Can you find the nine tables that have just one student?

Start

14

Finish

KEY

🍎 Lunch Counter ♻️ Recycling

🗑️ Trash Ⓣⓡ Tray Return

15

START

16

Field Day Frazzle

Get ready ... get set ... GO! If you're standing by the sign-up table, which direction do you have to go to get to the long jump? The obstacle course? The compass rose? Are the tug-of-war kids pulling north and south, or west and east?

FINISH

KEY

- Sign-up Table
- Award Stage
- Long Jump
- Obstacle Course
- 50-yard Dash
- Tug-of-war

Computer Confusion

With a **CLICK CLICK** here and a **CLICK CLICK** there ... Search for the girl in the striped shirt. Is she west or east of the teacher? Which direction is she from the guinea pig? The Finish?

START

4x3=12

3x5=_

ABC

9-6=_

18

8-5=_

6x4=_
5+10=_

7-4=_

FINISH

19

Baffled in Band

Make some music! TOODLE-E-DOO! How many instruments can you name? Can you spot all 11 drums? Is the piano west or east of the Start? Which is farther south—the guitar or the harp?

START

START

CLaY

22

The Heart of Art

Draw a daisy. Play with clay. What will you paint today? Use the key to find all five pottery stations. Which direction are they from the art supplies? Is the key north or south of the cleanup area?

FINISH

KEY

- Art Supplies
- Cleanup Area
- Kiln
- Pottery Station

START

24

Take a Bow!

The school play is just days away, and there's still so much to do! Are the costume racks west or east of the painters? Which is farther north—the car or the five-eyed monster? Can you find all 10 stage lights?

FINISH

MAZE ANSWERS
Hooray for Homeroom! (page 4-5)

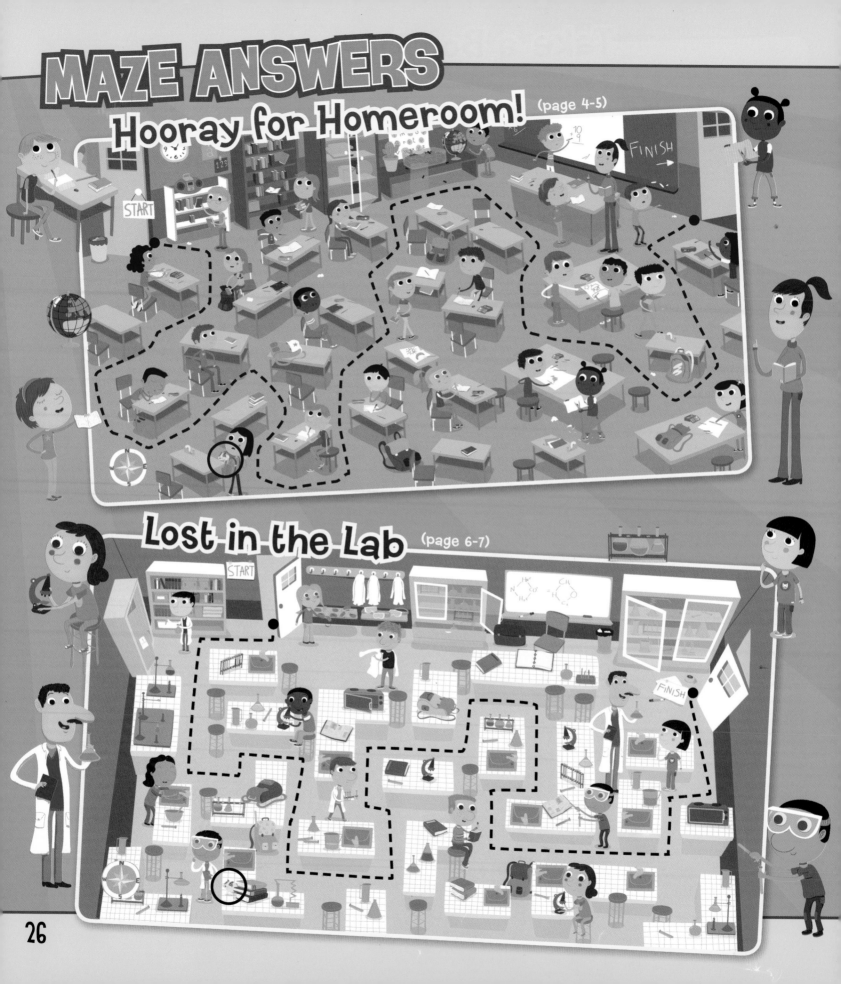

Lost in the Lab (page 6-7)

Read All about It (page 8-9)

START

FINISH

Balls, Walls, Nets, and Beams (page 10-11)

START

FINISH

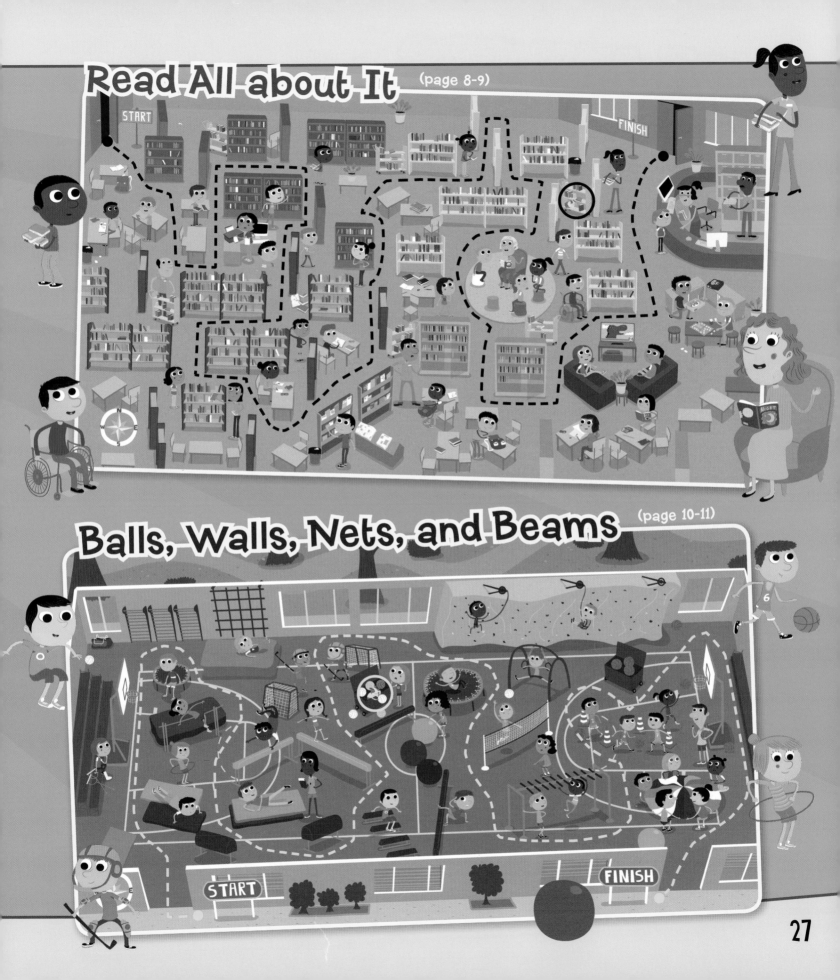

MAZE ANSWERS (continued)

Take Your Seat (page 12-13)

Who's Hungry? (page 14-15)

Field Day Frazzle
(page 16-17)

FINISH

START

Computer Confusion
(page 18-19)

START

FINISH

$4 \times 3 = 12$

$3 \times 5 =$

$9 - 6 =$

$8 - 5 =$

$6 + 6$, $5 = 18 =$

$7 - 4 =$

29

Baffled in Band (page 20-21)

The Heart of Art (page 22-23)

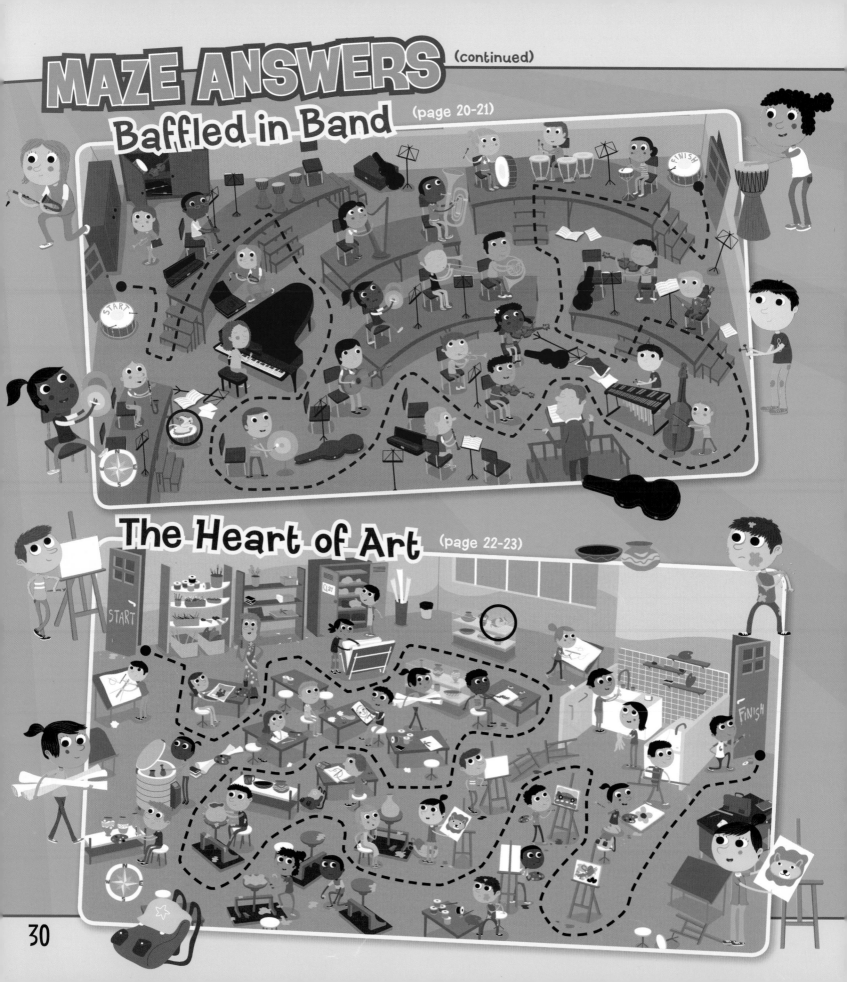

Take a Bow! (page 24-25)

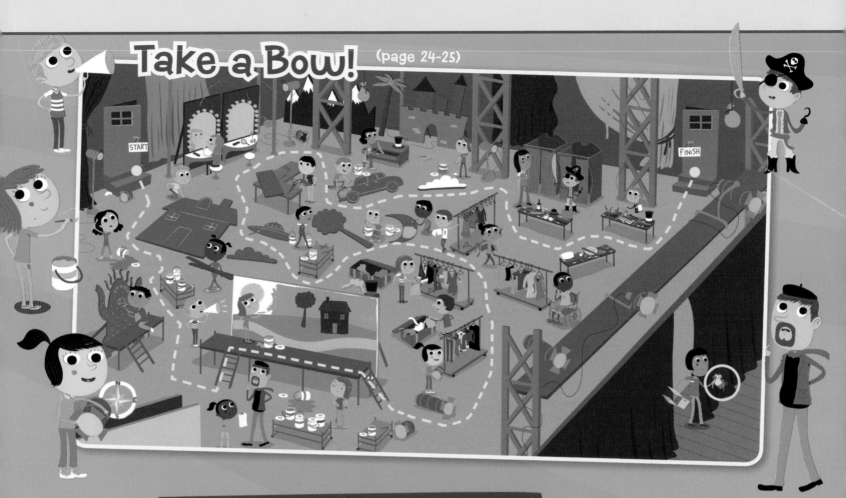

Guinea Pig Rules

1. Do not hide in backpacks.
2. Do not ride on book carts.
3. Do not hog all the balls.
4. Do not snack in the auditorium.
5. Do not jump on the drums.

TO LEARN MORE

More Books to Read

Blair, Beth L. *The Everything Kids' Gross Mazes Book: Wind Your Way Through Hours of Twisted Turns, Sick Shortcuts, and Disgusting Detours!* An Everything Series Book. Avon, Mass.: Adams Media, 2006.

Munro, Roxie. *Ecomazes: Twelve Earth Adventures.* New York: Sterling, 2010.

White, Graham. *Search for Pirate Treasure.* A Maze Adventure. Washington, D.C.: National Geographic, 2009.

Internet Sites

FactHound offers a safe, fun way to find Internet sites related to this book. All of the sites on FactHound have been researched by our staff.

Here's all you do:

Visit *www.facthound.com*

Type in this code: 9781404860391

Look for all the books in the A-MAZE-ing Adventures series: